SEMINOLE

Big Buddy Books
An Imprint of Abdo Publishing
www.abdopublishing.com

Sarah Tieck

www.abdopublishing.com

Published by Abdo Publishing, a division of ABDO, PO Box 398166, Minneapolis, Minnesota 55439.
Copyright © 2015 by Abdo Consulting Group, Inc. International copyrights reserved in all countries. No part
of this book may be reproduced in any form without written permission from the publisher. Big Buddy Books™
is a trademark and logo of Abdo Publishing.

Printed in the United States of America, North Mankato, Minnesota.
052014
092014

THIS BOOK CONTAINS
RECYCLED MATERIALS

Cover Photo: © NativeStock.com/AngelWynn.
Interior Photos: Getty Images (pp. 16, 25, 30); © Mary Evans Picture Library/Alamy (p. 19); National Geographic/
    Getty Images (pp. 5, 15, 17, 29); © NativeStock.com/AngelWynn (pp. 9, 17, 21); © North Wind/North Wind
    Picture Archives (pp. 13, 23, 25, 27); Shutterstock (pp. 11, 26).

Coordinating Series Editor: Rochelle Baltzer
Contributing Editors: Bridget O'Brien, Marcia Zappa
Graphic Design: Adam Craven

Library of Congress Cataloging-in-Publication Data

Tieck, Sarah, 1976-
  Seminole / Sarah Tieck.
     pages cm. -- (Native Americans)
  ISBN 978-1-62403-356-8
1. Seminole Indians--History--Juvenile literature. 2. Seminole Indians--Social life and customs--Juvenile literature.
I. Title.
  E99.S28T57 2014
  975.9004'973859--dc23
                              2014006315

CONTENTS

Amazing People 4

Seminole Territory 6

Home Life 8

What They Ate 10

Daily Life 12

Made by Hand 16

Spirit Life 18

Storytellers 20

Fighting for Land 22

Back in Time 26

A Strong Nation 28

Glossary 31

Websites 31

Index 32

Amazing People

Hundreds of years ago, North America was mostly wild, open land. Native Americans lived there. They had their own languages and **customs**.

The Seminole (SEH-muh-nohl) are a Native American nation. They are known for their long fight to **protect** their villages. Let's learn more about these Native Americans.

Did You Know?

Some people believe the name *Seminole* means "runaway." This came from a Creek Native American word. Others think it came from a Spanish word meaning "wild."

Traditional Seminole clothing includes bright, colorful patterns.

5

SEMINOLE TERRITORY

At first, the Seminole homelands were in parts of Alabama and southern Georgia. Beginning in the 1700s, the people started moving south into Florida.

Over time, the Seminole built villages in what is now known as the Everglades. Plants grew thick in these wetlands. This helped keep villages hidden. It **protected** the tribes from outsiders.

Did You Know?

The Seminole were originally part of the Creek tribe. They spoke a Muskogean language. They were known as Seminole after they moved to Florida.

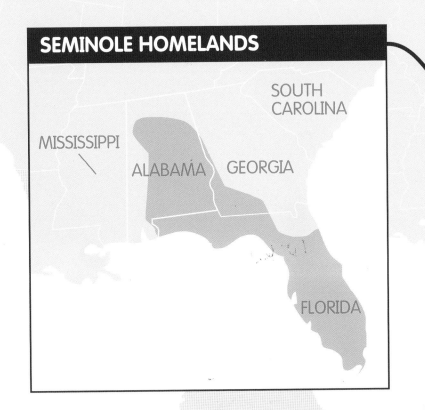

CANADA

UNITED STATES

SEMINOLE HOMELANDS

MISSISSIPPI

ALABAMA   GEORGIA

SOUTH
CAROLINA

FLORIDA

MEXICO

N
W E
S

HOME LIFE

Originally, the Seminole lived in log cabins. But when they moved to the Everglades, they began building chickees. These homes could be built quickly.

Chickee frames were made of strong cypress logs. These stood in the earth, raising the living space above the wetlands. The roof was made of palmetto leaves. They were held together by vines or ropes.

The Everglades can be very warm.
So, chickees had no walls.

What They Ate

The Seminole were hunters, gatherers, and farmers. The men hunted otters, raccoons, birds, alligators, deer, and turtles. They fished from canoes using spears. The tribe gathered wild pineapples and oranges. They planted corn and pumpkins.

Did You Know?

The Seminole made a drink called *Sofk* from corn. They used sugarcane to sweeten their foods.

The Everglades are rich with plants and animals. Sometimes, the Seminole caught and ate alligators!

Daily Life

Some Seminole villages were large. Most of them had a shared eating house. There, the women made food for the village.

The Seminole wore clothes made from parts of animals and plants. Men wore long shirts called tunics. Women wore long skirts and short shirts with capes. They decorated them with beautiful beads and bright cloth strips called patchwork.

In the 1800s, the Seminole shared in many tasks of daily living, such as cooking.

In a Seminole village, people had different jobs. Men hunted, fished, and fought off enemies. They served as tribe leaders. Women cared for the home and children. Men and women both served as storytellers and artists. Sometimes, they played a game called stickball.

The children learned everyday skills from their parents. Girls were taught to sew. Boys learned how to fish, hunt, and build canoes.

Stickball is a favorite game for tribe members.

MADE BY HAND

The Seminole made many objects by hand. They made tools, crafts, and clothes. These arts and crafts added beauty to their lives but were also useful.

Palmetto Dolls
The tribe made colorful dolls from palmetto plants. They had traditional Seminole clothing and hairstyles.

Patchwork

The Seminole sewed patterns and designs from cloth. Colorful patchwork can be found on dolls, clothes, and other items.

Handmade Baskets

Seminole people are known for making baskets from sweetgrass and palmetto. These plants grow in the Everglades. They are washed and dried, then sewn together. The baskets could be used to hold food and other items.

Dugout Canoes

The Seminole carved cypress logs into flat dugout canoes. They used wooden poles to steer and sometimes made sails.

SPIRIT LIFE

Religion was important to the Seminole. They believed in spiritual beings. These beings were fair and **consistent** with humans. The Seminole turned to **medicine men** for healing and help.

Ceremonies were an important part of the Seminole religion. One major ceremony was the Green Corn Dance. It was about becoming pure, seeking forgiveness, and finding **renewal**. It was also a social gathering.

The Green Corn Dance took place in the spring. The Seminole performed stomp dancing and other activities. Some Seminole still perform the ceremony today.

19

STORYTELLERS

Before the Seminole had written words, they told stories to teach people about their history. They also shared ideas about living in nature and why the world is the way it is. Stories were sometimes told at the beginning of **ceremonies**. Being a storyteller was a great honor.

Did You Know?

Elders told stories to children at night around a campfire. These stories were often about Rabbit, Corn Lady, Deer Girl, and other Everglades creatures.

Today, stomp dancing and storytelling are often part of the same events.

21

Fighting for Land

Land was important to the Seminole. In the 1700s, the tribe moved to Florida. This area was ruled by the Spanish. The Seminole built homes deep in forested wetlands now known as the Everglades.

In the late 1700s, the Seminole helped some American **slaves** who had escaped. They also fought with American settlers. So in 1817, the US Army and Seminole began fighting the First Seminole War. The Seminole lost in 1818.

 The First Seminole War was fought when US
soldiers tried to catch and return escaped slaves.

By 1819, the United States began ruling Florida. The government wanted the Seminole to move west to Indian Territory in what is now Oklahoma. The Seminole wanted to stay on their homelands. They fought two more wars. Many people died, and the wars were costly.

Over time, many Seminole moved to Oklahoma **reservations**. The remaining Florida Seminole continued to fight for land and other rights. Today, many live on reservations in Florida.

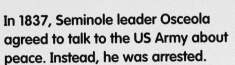 In 1837, Seminole leader Osceola agreed to talk to the US Army about peace. Instead, he was arrested.

 The Second Seminole War was fought from 1835 to 1842. The Third Seminole War was fought from 1855 to 1858.

BACK IN TIME

1700s

The Seminole moved to Florida. At this time, it was ruled by the Spanish.

1817

The Seminole began fighting with the United States in the First Seminole War. It ended in 1818.

1838

Seminole leader Osceola died in prison. His people were fighting in the Second Seminole War. The war had started in 1835 and would last seven years.

1855

The Third Seminole War began. It ended in 1858.

1970

The Indian Claims Commission gave the Seminole $12,347,500. This was to pay them for the Florida land that the US Army took from them.

2010

The US government counted about 14,000 Seminole living in the country.

A Strong Nation

The Seminole people have a long, rich history. They are remembered for fighting to keep their Florida homelands. They are also known for their colorful **traditional** clothing.

Seminole roots run deep. Today, the people have kept alive those special things that make them Seminole. Even though times have changed, many people carry the traditions, stories, and memories of the past into the present.

Today, many Seminole live in Oklahoma. Some remain in Florida.

29

"Let our last sleep be in the graves of our native land!"

— Osceola

GLOSSARY

ceremony a formal event on a special occasion.
consistent being unchanging in actions or beliefs.
custom a practice that has been around a long time and is common to a group or a place.
medicine man a Native American healer and spiritual leader.
protect (pruh-TEHKT) to guard against harm or danger.
renewal the state of being made new or fresh again.
reservation (reh-zuhr-VAY-shuhn) a piece of land set aside by the government for Native Americans to live on.
slave a person who is bought and sold as property.
traditional (truh-DIHSH-nuhl) relating to a tradition, which is a belief, a custom, or a story handed down from older people to younger people.

WEBSITES

To learn more about Native Americans, visit **booklinks.abdopublishing.com**. These links are routinely monitored and updated to provide the most current information available.

INDEX

arts and crafts **12, 14, 16, 17**

canoes **10, 14, 17**

chickees **8, 9**

clothing **5, 12, 16, 17, 28**

Creek **4, 6**

Everglades **6, 8, 9, 11, 17, 20, 22**

farming **10**

fishing **10, 14**

food **10, 11, 12, 17**

Green Corn Dance **18, 19**

homelands **6, 22, 24, 26, 28, 29**

hunting **10, 11, 14**

language **4, 6**

log cabins **8**

Osceola **25, 26, 30**

religion **18, 19**

reservations **24**

Seminole Wars **22, 23, 24, 25, 26, 27**

Spain **4, 22, 26**

stickball **14, 15**

stomp dancing **19, 21**

stories **14, 20, 21, 28**

United States **22, 23, 24, 25, 26, 27**